*Editor:* Nicholas De Vere
*Designer:* Andrew Wilkinson
*Picture researcher:* Emma Krikler
*Illustrator:* Ron Hayward Associates

© Aladdin Books 1991

*First published in
the USA in 1991 by*
Franklin Watts Inc.
387 Park Avenue South
New York NY 10016

Library of Congress Cataloging-in-Publication Data

Cross, Robin.
    Modern military weapons / by Robin Cross.
       p. cm.
    Includes index.
    Summary: Examines today's modern weapons of land,
air, and sea; with special emphasis on the high tech
"smart" bombs and missiles.
    ISBN 0-531-15627-3. -- ISBN 0-531-11174-1
    (lib. bdg.)
    1. Weapons systems--Juvenile literature. 2.
Munitions--Juvenile literature. [1. Weapons
systems. 2. Munitions.] I. Title.
UF500.C76 1991
355.8'2--dc20          91-12317  CIP     AC

Printed in Belgium

# MODERN MILITARY WEAPONS

# ROBIN CROSS

# CONTENTS

# INTRODUCTION

Since the destruction of the Japanese cities of Hiroshima and Nagasaki by atomic bombs in August 1945 there has been a new industrial revolution in military weapons. The awesome build-up of nuclear weaponry by the U.S.A. and the Soviet Union during the 1960s and 1970s has finally led to agreements to reduce the number of warheads on both sides. At the same time the recent Gulf War brought together a complete new range of conventional weaponry, much of which had previously been unused in combat. Microelectronics and computer science have not only reshaped our daily lives, but have also revolutionized the battlefield, which now extends upwards from the infantryman on the ground to missile systems and military satellites orbiting the earth in space.

Nowadays new inventions in microelectronics are often the work of military scientists and find their first application in weapons systems, particularly warships, tanks, combat aircraft, and missiles. Surveillance systems (which find, identify, and track the enemy), missile guidance, and warhead design have all undergone radical development.

All this costs a great deal of money. For example, the computerized fire-control system at the heart of a modern main battle tank accounts for about 20 percent of its total cost. Throughout the 1980s expenditure on electronics made up at least one third of the equipment costs of the United States Air Force (USAF).

The development of microelectronics has gone hand in hand with advances in many other technologies to produce a range of new materials from laminated armor to fiber optics; more powerful engines and more efficient fuels; and smaller, lighter, precision-guided weapons delivered from increasingly adaptable platforms. When dealing with modern military systems, less often means more. For instance, four fully loaded F-16 fighters can pack a punch as big and far more accurately than an entire World War II bombardment group of 24 B-17 heavy bombers.

One of the most important aspects of modern warfare is the enormous increase in the destructive power of conventional munitions. A dramatic example is provided by the Multiple-Launch Rocket System (MLRS) employed by the coalition forces in the Gulf War. Just one MLRS salvo has a destructive power equivalent to a small nuclear weapon. The MLRS is a massively expensive system, but its total cost represents just a fraction of the figure of over $100,000 million a year invested worldwide in military research and development.

◁ Black Hawk helicopter lowers a 105mm M102 lightweight howitzer during an exercise of the U.S. 101st Airborne Division.

3

# LAND POWER

*For the last 50 years the main battle tank has provided the cutting edge of land power. Although vulnerable to antitank missiles, ground-attack aircraft, and attack helicopters, the most potent enemy of a tank remains another tank.*

## MAIN BATTLE TANKS

At the heart of main battle tank (MBT) design are highly efficient engines, which allow for heavy armor and generate great speeds and long range. Modern tanks are armed with extremely powerful guns. They carry a "mix" of ammunition: high explosive ammunition for use against lightly protected vehicles and "soft" targets, and one or more types of armor-piercing ammunition.

The most effective armor for the modern tank is the British-developed Chobham armor. This has layers of aluminum, ceramics, steel, and other materials to absorb the large amounts of kinetic energy delivered by antitank munitions and the heat produced when the warheads of modern antitank munitions explode.

Tank gunnery has undergone dramatic changes since 1945. Laser range finders and sights, computerized fire-control systems (which can measure and correct for such variables as wind speed, air humidity and barrel wear) and fully stabilized armament give a high degree of accuracy.

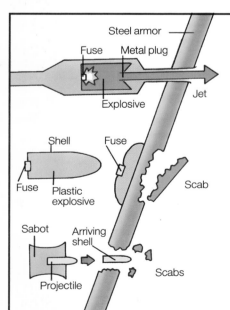

## ANTITANK AMMUNITION

**HEAT** (High Explosive Antitank) round: jet of molten metal pierces armor up to five times warhead diameter

**HESH** (High Explosive Squash-Head) round: crumples on impact, then explosive is detonated. Deadly scabs of armor are blasted into tank

**APDS** (Armor-Piercing Discarding Sabot) round: armor is pierced by depleted uranium round which discards sabot as round leaves barrel

△ The German Leopard 2, whose design incorporates advanced Chobham-type armor which provides complete protection against some types of antitank weapons, and against others is nearly twice as effective as conventional armor. The first of the new generation of MBTs to enter service, in 1978, the Leopard combines the three vital elements in tank design – mobility, firepower and protection. **Crew**: 4 **Road speed**: 42mph **Range**: 330mi **Armament**: 120mm gun, two 7.62mm machine guns, eight smoke dischargers each side of turret.

The main Soviet MBT is the T-72 (not shown here). It is a formidable tank with a powerful 125mm smoothbore gun fitted with an alloy thermal jacket, firing fin-stablized ammunition of several types. **Crew**: 3 **Road speed**: 37mph **Range**: 300mi **Armament**: 125mm gun, one 7.62mm and one 12.7mm machine gun.

▷ The Challenger, latest MBT to join the British Army with first combat role in the Gulf. Its night observation equipment, known as TOGS (Thermal Observation and Gunnery System) enables the crew to fight in total darkness. **Crew**:4 **Road Speed**: 35mph **Range**: 370mi **Armament**: 120mm gun, 27.62mm machine guns, one bank of six smoke dischargers on each side of turret.

▷ The U.S. M1A1 Abrams, seen here in the Gulf during Operation Desert Shield, engine is powered by a gas-turbine engine. The tank's laser range finder is coupled to a fully stabilized sight and linked to an onboard digital computer. **Crew**: 4 **Road speed**: 42mph **Range**: 300mi **Armament**: 120mm gun, one 12.7mm and two 7.62mm machine guns, six smoke dischargers on each side of turret.

## ARMORED FIGHTING VEHICLES

The main battle tank is only one of many different types of armored fighting vehicle. Others perform specialized tasks: tracked and wheeled reconnaissance vehicles gather information before the main battle tanks advance; combat engineer vehicles, usually based on an obsolete main battle tank chassis, are equipped to perform many tasks on the battlefield, including clearing obstacles and minefields, building and repair of roads, and bridging water obstacles; and Mechanized Infantry Combat Vehicles (MICVs) carry troops into battle.

In battle, tanks need the support of both artillery and infantry, whose principal task is to deal with enemy infantry who are armed with antitank missiles. In a mobile armored battle speed and flexibility are the key words. Infantry no longer have to march behind tanks. They now move at speed in heavily armored fighting vehicles which carry their own tactical weapon systems.

In the early 1960s the Soviet Union led the way in the development of MICVs, introducing the BMP-1, which can carry eight men, is equipped with extensive Nuclear, Biological, Chemical (NBC) protection and is armed with a 30mm cannon and wire-guided antitank missiles. Subsequent Western equivalents include the German Marder, the French AMX-10P, the American M2A2 Bradley and the British MCV-80 Warrior. The Bradley has a seven-man infantry squad in the fighting compartment.

▽ The British Warrior Mechanized Infantry Combat Vehicle, which entered service in 1987. The Warrior carries seven fully equipped infantry and a crew of three (commander, gunner and driver). Although Warrior's fighting compartment contains air filters, a chemical lavatory and even electric kettles, the infantrymen still have a rough ride. They cannot see where they are going, as there are no windows, and when travelling at full speed they are prey to nausea akin to seasickness. As soon as the back door opens the infantrymen are in battle, and drills for high-speed exiting of the MICV are essential. The Warrior is armed with a 30mm Rardon cannon which can fire 900 armor-piercing rounds a minute and can defeat light armored vehicles like the Soviet BMP-2, and a 7.62mm machine gun. **Crew**: 3+7 **Road speed**: 45mph **Range**: 310mi **Armament**: 30mm cannon, one 7.62 machine gun, four smoke dischargers on each side of turret.

◁ The M2 Bradley, which is larger and more heavily armed than the British Warrior. The Bradley has a full range of night vision devices, an NBC system and is amphibious. There is a rear power-operated ramp. **Crew**: 3+7 **Road speed**: 40mph **Range**: 288mi **Armament**: 25mm cannon, 7.62mm machine gun, twin launcher for seven TOW antitank missiles, four smoke dischargers on each side of turret.

◁ Unlike the Bradley, the Warrior has no firing ports for its infantry, although periscopes are fitted to aid surveillance. During the development of Warrior a decision was made to emphasize mobility and protection over firepower, and as a result missile armament was rejected on the grounds that it would provide a distraction from Warrior's primary role. The commander and gunner sit in the turret and the driver in the left front of the hull.

An armored bridgelayer, based on the chassis of a British Chieftain MBT, with a scissors-type assault bridge. Assault engineers must operate in the heart of the battle, preserving the freedom of maneuver of their own forces, providing them with protective construction and hampering the maneuver of enemy forces in areas where fire and maneuver can be used to destroy him. To achieve this modern armies deploy a wide range of specialized equipment, including armored engineer assault vehicles, armored bulldozers and earthmovers, minelayers and clearers and armored equipment for the recovery of disabled vehicles which have been disabled on the battlefield.

# LAND POWER

## ARTILLERY

Field artillery performs a number of roles. It supports troops and armor by pinning down the enemy, destroying their defensive positions and equipment and preventing them from moving across the battlefield. Long-range artillery is used to disrupt the enemy's lines of communication to his forward positions, halting the movement of men, supplies and armored formations before they reach the front line. Counter-battery artillery is tasked with the destruction of enemy artillery.

Much of today's field artillery is self-propelled, and able to move at greater speed in a high-intensity battlefield than traditional towed artillery. The new generation of self-propelled (SP) artillery is almost as sophisticated as the modern main battle tank, boasting computerized fire control, automated ammunition handling and purpose-built chassis design. The Soviet Union retains a mix of SP and towed artillery but almost all U.S. front-line artillery is self-propelled. Its heaviest weapon is the 203mm M110A2 howitzer, which can fire a wide range of nuclear, chemical, high-explosive and Improved Conventional Munitions (ICMs). Nevertheless, the U.S. Marine Corps still uses a high proportion of towed artillery, notably the light 155mm M198 howitzer.

△ The 155mm M198 howitzer, the U.S. Marine Corps' standard towed weapon, which can fire nuclear ammunition. On a howitzer the projectile and propelling charge are loaded separately, so that the size of the charge can be varied for different ranges and targets. The howitzer can fire at an angle of high elevation to deliver plunging fire vertically on to the target. Projectiles that can be fired include high explosive, illuminating, rocket assisted explosive, carrier shell containing antitank mines, antipersonnel bomblets, and nuclear.

◁ The British 105mm gun, which has a range of 55,750ft and is capable of firing a shell every 10 seconds. Carried by helicopter, it can be ready for action within 90 seconds of touchdown. In the Falklands War of 1982 its mobility and spread of fire used to complement the high velocity and rate of fire of the naval gunfire.

▷ The U.S. 155mm M109 SP howitzer is widely used by Western armies, and over 4,000 have been produced since 1961. It is based on a tracked chassis specially developed for the purpose of a self-propelled gun, and is constructed with aluminum armor. The M109 uses its main vehicle engine to power its systems and the turret can rotate through 360 degrees, enabling rapid switching of targets. The ammunition and crew are housed in the welded aluminum turret, which provides shell splinter and NBC protection. The gun is also fitted with a muzzle brake and fume extractor. Maximum range is 78,750ft. Each U.S. Army armored and mechanized division fields 54 M109s, which can fire a wide range of ammunition including tactical nuclear.

The U.S. Multiple Launch Rocket System (MLRS). Modern armies employ rocket artillery as "area weapons," whose relative innacuracy is offset by their great destructive power and psychological effect. Most rockets are simple, inexpensive weapons fired over a relatively short range from truck-mounted launcher tubes or racks. But the MLRS, which is also used by the UK, Italy, France, West Germany, the Netherlands and the army of South Korea is a costly precision long-range weapon with a tracked high-mobility chassis and range of over 18mi. Its launcher fires ripples of unguided 277mm rockets carrying antitank or antipersonnel submunitions which can plaster an area 27,000ft square. The MLRS was used to great effect in the opening phase of the Gulf War against the Iraqi divisions holding Kuwait.

## INFANTRY

Infantry now ride into battle in helicopters and Mechanized Infantry Combat Vehicles (MICVs), and carry lighter and more compact weapons. The standard assault rifle of the U.S. infantry is the M16A2 of 5.56mm caliber. Equivalents are the Soviet AK-74 (a development of the famous AK-47), the French FA MAS and the British L85 Individual Weapon. These can be adjusted for full or semiautomatic fire, can carry a magazine of around 30-45 rounds and have an effective range of 985-1,640ft.

Also carried by the infantry are General Purpose Machine Guns (GPMGs) such as the U.S. M60 which can be fired from a tripod or from the hip, or light machine guns (LMGs) such as the Soviet 7.62mm RPK. Heavy machine guns (HMGs) fire rounds of heavier caliber than a rifle but below 20mm. The usual caliber of these weapons is 12.7mm, and they are often mounted on tactical vehicles or specialist antiaircraft mounts. Mortars are smooth-bore, muzzle-loaded, short-barrelled weapons firing a fin-stabilized bomb. Light, simple, cheap to manufacture, and capable of a rapid rate of fire, mortars are particularly effective in close infantry fighting and are in particular much used by the Soviet Union.

The British SA-80, or Enfield Weapon System, has two parts. Pictured here is the L85 Individual Weapon, a 5.56mm combat rifle. It is complemented by the L86 Light Support Weapon, a light machine gun with the same layout, longer barrel and folding bipod, designed to provide longer-range support fire for infantry sections.

◁ The Brandt 120mm mortar, which has a rifled barrel and a maximum rocket-assisted range of 42,650ft. This model is resting on its baseplate and travelling wheels for firing. These provide extra stability and enable the mortar to be deployed very rapidly. In spite of its size, the Brandt 120mm is still muzzle-loaded by hand with bombs which weigh approximately 42lb. In addition to mortars, infantrymen are equipped with a variety of "human-portable" missiles. They include the Soviet AT-3 "Sagger" and Euromissile Milan wire-guided antitank missiles and the American Stinger infrared-guided shoulder-launched surface-to-air missile (SAM), designed to deal with low-altitude high-speed jet aircraft or helicopters. Simple and robust, the Stinger proved very effective in the hands of Afghan guerrillas.

△ A TOW (Tube-Launched Optically Tracked Wire Guided) anti-tank missile mounted on a U.S. Humvee general-purpose vehicle. The operator of the BGM-71 TOW keeps the target in the crosshairs of his sight while its flight is controlled by electronic guidance signals transmitted down two very fine wires unspooling from the missile. The TOW is the West's most widely used guided anti-tank weapon.

The U.S. M60 General Purpose Machine Gun, dubbed "The Pig" by troops in Vietnam because of its weight and unreliability. Too heavy to be an effective light machine gun and with too light a barrel for a sustained-fire role for long periods when tripod-mounted, the M60 is now being replaced as the U.S. armed forces' Squad Automatic Weapon (SAW) by the M249, based on the Belgian FN Minimi.

# AIR POWER

*In its pure form the fighter is an aircraft designed solely for the destruction of other aircraft. Since the early 1960s, however, fighters not only keep the skies clear of enemy aircraft, but are also adapted to deliver gunfire, bombs, and other munitions.*

## FIGHTERS

The McDonnell Douglas F-4 Phantom, which began its service life in 1960 as a carrier-based all-weather air superiority fighter, was used in a strategic bombing role in the Vietnam War. It entered the 1990s as a multirole fighter for ship or land operations, an all-weather multisensor reconnaissance aircraft and defense suppression aircraft. The advanced aerodynamic techniques incorporated into the General Dynamics F-16 Fighting Falcon, which entered service in 1978, enables it to carry a weapons load of up to 20,500lb.

In combat, agility and maneuverability are vital to survival. In the latest generation of fighters agility and maneuverability are enhanced by "relaxed stability" flowing from "fly-by-wire" (FBW) control. Previously all aircraft needed a measure of inbuilt stability to allow pilots to retain control. Now, by using an inherently unstable airframe controlled by a computer, the fighter is highly maneuverable.

△ The General Dynamics F-16 Fighting Falcon, an immensely maneuverable multirole fighter, seen here in its attack role. This F-16A of the USAF's 388th Tactical Fighter Wing is carrying two types of Sidewinder AAM, two 2,000lb bombs, two ferry tanks and, at the root of the right wing, an ALQ-119 jamming pod. **Speed**: 1,285mph (at high level) **Range**: 2,420mi **Ceiling**: 50,000ft **Armament**: (fighter role) one M61 20mm six-barreled cannon, two or four Sidewinder AAMs, two Sparrow or medium-range AMRAAM missiles.

▽ The McDonnell Douglas F-15 Eagle, designed as an uncompromised air superiority fighter but also effective in the tactical attack role. **Speed**: 1,600mph (at high level) **Range**: 2,778mi **Ceiling**: 60,400ft **Armament**: one M61 20mm cannon, four Sidewinder and four Sparrow AAMs.

▷ The Soviet Mikoyan Gurevich Mig-29 "Fulcrum," which lacks the aerodynamic elegance of the F-16, but comes close to matching its overall performance and agility. Like its Western counterparts, it is equipped with "look-down" radar and "shoot-down" missiles that can seek out targets from above.
**Speed**: 1,520mph (at high level)
**Range**: 1,300 mi **Ceiling**: 55,750ft
**Armament**: one 30mm cannon, plus combination of AA-10 "Alamo" and AA-11 "Archer" AAMs.

▷ The French Dassault-Breguet Mirage 2000C entered service in 1984 and combines a delta wing with "relaxed" stability, "fly-by-wire" control system and pulse-Doppler radar. It carries two short-range (max 6mi) Matra R.550 AAMs on the outboard pylons and two longer range (max 21mi) Matra Super 530 AAMs inboard **Speed**: 1,320mph (at high level) **Range**: 2,070mi **Ceiling**: 59,000ft **Armament**: Two 30mm cannon, two Matra Super 530, two Matra 550 AAMs.

## BOMBERS

Large strategic bombers have the slowest rate of change, and the longest lives, of any type of military aircraft. The USAF's Boeing B-52 Stratofortress was designed in 1948 to deliver free-fall nuclear bombs over great distances. In the Gulf War, it reverted to the tactical role it had played for much of the Vietnam War, carpet-bombing Iraqi troop concentrations with conventional "iron bombs."

Six billion dollars were spent on the four prototypes of the B-52's sucessor, the Rockwell International B-1B, which entered service in 1986. Designed to combine the B-52's range with the performance of the General Dynamics FB-111A medium-range strategic bomber variant of the F-111 fighter-bomber, the B-1B has been aptly described as a huge computer system surrounded by fuel and engines. The 186-ton B-1B is equipped to fly under hostile air defense surveillance radar at high subsonic speed about 230ft above the ground. Each one costs about $210 million.

▷ A Boeing B-52G releases an AGM-109 medium-range air-to-surface missile (MRASM), a variant of the Tomahawk cruise missile. With a range of 285mi the AGM-109 is armed with a payload of "area denial" submunitions. Armed with air-launched cruise missiles (ALCMs),the B-52 now has a low-level stand-off role, exploiting advanced avionics to penetrate the war zone at tree-top height. The B-52 retains formidable firepower in an ageing airframe. **Speed**: 595mph **Range**: 7,500mi **Ceiling**: 55,000lb **Armament**: max of 50,700lb weapons inc. 12ALCMs, free-fall weapons; four 12.7mm guns in tail turret.

◁ The Rockwell B-1B is designed to penetrate hostile airspace at low level and high subsonic speed. It is equipped with terrain-following radar and its variable-geometry wings sweep back to smooth out the bumps of a low-level ride while small vanes in its nose detect gusts and turbulence and direct the main control surfaces. Packed with sophisticated avionics, the B-1B has nevertheless been plagued by mechanical problems. **Speed**: 800mph (at high level), 600mph (low level) **Range**: 7,200mi **Armament**: max of eight ALCMs internally and 14 externally; 24 SRAMs and free-fall weapons; max conventional load of 75,900lb.

◁ The Soviet Tupolev Tu-26 "Backfire" strategic bomber, which serves with both the air force and the navy, the latter employing its "Backfires" mostly on antiship operations. **Speed**: 1,320mph (at high level) **Range**: 6,800mi **Ceiling**: 62,335ft **Armament**: twin 23mm cannon in tail; up to three AS-4 or A-6 cruise missiles or 26,455lb of stores.

## STEALTH

The angular shape of the Lockheed F-117A fighter-bomber is dictated by its stealth technology. Ungainly and subsonic, it is built of radar-absorbent materials while its basic shape of flat surfaces scatters radar beams, making it extremely difficult to detect. Its radar-eluding shape makes it inherently unstable and the pilot uses "fly-by-wire" computers and fiber optics to control the aircraft. It can carry two 2,000lb laser-guided bombs, one of which was among the first bombs to be dropped on Baghdad at the start of the Gulf War.

## ATTACK/STRIKE

"Attack" aircraft are used against surface forces and installations close to the front line or in the rear of the battlefield. Examples of such aircraft are the U.S. A10A Thunderbolt II, the British Harrier GR Mk3 and Soviet Sukhoi Su-25 Frogfoot. Also flying tactical missions, but capable of penetrating deeper into the war zone and attacking targets with tactical nuclear weapons, "strike" aircraft like the American General Dynamics F-111, the Anglo-French SEPECAT Jaguar, Soviet Sukhoi Su-24 "Fencer" and the Panavia Tornado GR Mk1.

▷ The Tornado, a strike aircraft with a heavy all-weather punch. Its variable-geometry wing enables the Tornado to take off with a heavy load and wings swept forward and then, with the aid of terrain-following radar, fly low and fast to the target with wings swept back. **Speed**: 1,675mph (at high level) **Range**: 2,415mi **Armament**: two 27mm cannon and up to 19,840lb of stores, including JP 233 cratering system; nuclear capable.

◁ The A-10 Thunderbolt II, a formidable tank-killer dubbed the "Warthog" because of its ungainly appearance. Note the formidable 30mm cannon mounted ahead of the cockpit below the fuselage. **Speed**: 424mph **Range**: 2,369mi **Armament**: 30mm cannon, max of 15,968lb of externally carried stores, including Maverick ASMs.

### Electronic Warfare Aircraft

The effectiveness of modern weapons systems depends on the ability to concentrate devastating force in time and place at high speed and long range and with the minimum of human error. Modern war is fought on an electronic battlefield, and electronics lie at the heart of both the sophisticated command and control systems which bring weapons to bear and the weapons themselves. Significantly, electronics take up at least one-third of the USAF's equipment costs.

▽ The USAF's Lockheed TR-1A high-altitude reconnaisssance aircraft, whose Advanced Synthetic Aperture Radar System (ASARS) produces a fine-grain printout of everything within 34mi to one side of its flight path. **Speed**: 495mph **Range**: 2,200mi **Ceiling**: 90,000ft.

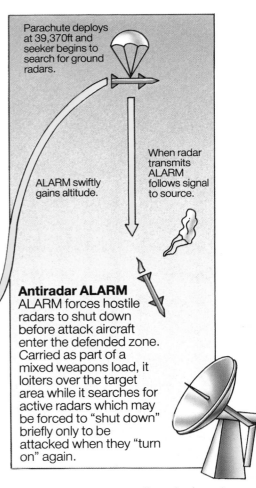

Parachute deploys at 39,370ft and seeker begins to search for ground radars.

ALARM swiftly gains altitude.

When radar transmits ALARM follows signal to source.

**Antiradar ALARM**
ALARM forces hostile radars to shut down before attack aircraft enter the defended zone. Carried as part of a mixed weapons load, it loiters over the target area while it searches for active radars which may be forced to "shut down" briefly only to be attacked when they "turn on" again.

Ground radar system

Tornado releases ALARM missile at low level.

The Tornado above is armed with the BAe Air-Launched Anti-Radiation Missile (ALARM), which hangs from a parachute until it finds an active transmitter. In a typical Gulf War attack on an Iraqi airfield the way for the ALARM-armed Tornados was paved by U.S. electronic warfare aircraft, EA-6B Prowlers and EF-111A Ravens, whose task was to blind Iraqi air defense radars. Then a wave of Tornados released their ALARMs at low level while a second wave swept in to strafe the airfield with the JP 233 runway attack system. High-level cover was provided by F-15 and Tornado F.Mk 3 fighters.

▷ The Boeing E-3 Sentry Airborne Warning and Control System (AWACS) aircraft. Its radar aerials are housed in the rotodome and can scan the airspace from ground level to the stratosphere. Tasked with identifying hostile aircraft and controlling friendly ones, the E-3 can stay aloft for over 20 hours with air refueling.

▷ The USAF's EF-111A Raven, a variant of the F-111 developed for electronic warfare. Equipped with the powerful AN/ALQ-99 tactical jamming system, its task is to blind hostile radars, creating a "jamming corridor" down which an attacking force can fly. It can also fly defensive missions, jamming the radars of intruding aircraft.

## ATTACK HELICOPTER

The helicopter has now evolved into a powerful weapons platform, carrying rockets, missiles and cannon and capable of seeking out and destroying enemy targets, including armor. The American Bell AH-1S Cobra, British Westland Lynx, as well as the Soviet Mil Mi-24 "Hind" are all examples of heavily armed machines that deliver great fire power.

In the early 1960s the U.S. Army drew up a specification for a dedicated armed escort and attack helicopter. Twenty years of development and many billions of dollars of investment led to the introduction, in 1985, of the McDonnell Douglas AH-64A Apache, which performed with success in the Gulf War.

▽ The Soviet Mil Mi-24 "Hind", one of the most powerfully armed helicopters in the world. Its stub wings confer high speed and excellent weapons lift, but the Hind's size and lack of maneuverability make it vulnerable on the battlefield. **Speed**: 200mph **Range**: 217mi **Ceiling**: 14,760ft **Armament**: nose-mounted four-barrelled 12.7mm gun; wing pylons usually carry four AT-2 "Swatter" antitank missiles (ATMs) and four rocket pods.

▽ A Westland Lynx of the British Army in desert color scheme. The TOW missile is its main weapon, and its roomy cabin can accommodate up to eight troops, making it an all-round weapon in the battlefield. **Speed**: 200mph **Range**: 335mi **Armament**: 20mm gun, eight TOW missiles.

▽ The business end of the Bell AH-1S Cobra. The weapons officer sits in the front of the cockpit and the pilot at the rear. Note the slim cross section. **Speed**: 140mph **Range**: 315mi **Ceiling**: 12,200ft **Armament**: eight TOW missiles on outboard stations with rocket or gun pods on inboard pylons and 20mm three-barrelled cannon.

## APACHE

The McDonnell Douglas AH-64A Apache, which performed impressively in the Gulf War, is a complex and expensive tank-killer which can fight in bad weather and darkness. Its advanced target acquisition systems can see the enemy through the fog of battle and then mark them with laser designation for the Apache's "fire-and-forget" Hellfire missiles. The Apache can also engage targets with its belly-mounted 30mm chain gun or unguided 70mm rockets, seen here on the outboard pylons. Its engines are heavily shrouded against heat emissions to counter heat-seeking missiles and its entire structure is built to withstand heavy ground fire. Mounted in a rotating turret in the nose, and coupled to the copilot/gunner's position, the Apache's target acquisition/ designation sight (TADS) provides a search, detection, and recognition capability using a combination of direct-view optics, television, or forward-looking infrared (FLIR). **Speed**: 180mph **Range**: 380mi **Ceiling**: 11,480ft **Armament**: 16 Hellfire ATM missiles, 70mm rockets, 30mm cannon.

The pilot's night vision sensor (PNVS) consists of forward-looking infrared sensor (FLIR) system mounted above the TADS, an electronics unit and the pilot's display and controls. Coordinated with the pilot's helmet display, the system allows the Apache to be flown in a "nap of the earth" profile around ground obstructions while simultaneously producing target information. Both Apache crew members are equipped with the IHADSS (integrated helmet and display sighting system).

Like the A-10's Maverick missile, the Hellfire homes on to a ground target illuminated by laser energy. Thus, unlike the TOW missile, it is not limited to line-of-sight attacks. Once its laser seeker has locked on to the target the Hellfire will strike home, even if the Apache is flying on a different heading. The Hellfire will steer toward a target illuminated by the Apache's own designator, a ground designator or that of another helicopter. The Hellfires can be launched in "ripples," fractions of a second apart but at different targets, selected by different designators on different pulsed codes.

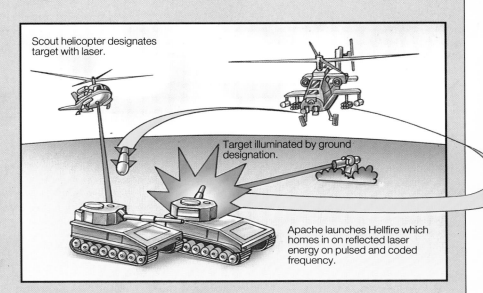

Scout helicopter designates target with laser.

Target illuminated by ground designation.

Apache launches Hellfire which homes in on reflected laser energy on pulsed and coded frequency.

## TRANSPORT

Most of the air forces in the world contain squadrons dedicated to military transport. The aircraft which changed the face of military transport was the Lockheed C-130 Hercules, introduced in 1956 and incorporating a wide range of new features and technologies. Today the Hercules remains in use worldwide and is the backbone of the USAF's tactical air transport squadrons. The bulk of the strategic (long-range) airlift of U.S. Military Airlift Command (MAC) is now handled by the Lockheed C-5 Galaxy, which entered service in 1970.

In the Soviet Union little distinction is made between military and civil transport. Aeroflot, the state carrier, is fully intergrated with V-TA, the Soviet equivalent of MAC. Shortage of prepared airfields in Siberia and the Third World have produced a range of Soviet transports designed for rough-strip short takeoff and landing operations, with high power-to-weight ratios, multiwheel undercarriages, adjustable tyre pressure and rocket-assisted takeoff notably the Antonov An-12 "Cub" and An-124 "Condor".

▷ The Lockheed C-5 Galaxy, backbone of American strategic airlift, which can carry the heaviest hardware items on a global basis. The Galaxy's entire nose hinges upward and a ramp is lowered to reveal the gaping interior and rear ramp doors which can be lowered to make a straight-through cargo hold. Its landing gear consists of 28 wheels which provide the "high flotation" needed for unpaved surfaces. A Galaxy's typical load can vary from two main battle tanks to five M113 armored personnel carriers. The great stress placed on the Galaxy's wings led to the decision in 1978 to rewing the entire C-5 fleet. **Speed**: 570mph **Range**: 6,465mi **Ceiling**: 35,740ft **Max payload**: 261,000lb.

◁ A Boeing Vertol CH-47 Chinook lifts a Scorpion light tank. The Chinook is the world's most successful heavy lift helicopter, operational with many air forces. In the Falklands War a single Chinook performed prodigious feats, at one point carrying 80 fully equipped troops, nearly double its official maximum of 44. The useful load of a CH-47D is 22,780lb. The CH-47 operates behind the front line, while assault helicopters like the Sikorsky UH-60A Black Hawk are tasked with carrying troops to critical points in the battle zone, resupplying them, and evacuating casualties. Rotary-wing aircraft, may be fuel-hungry, difficult to maintain, slower than fixed-wing aircraft and vulnerable on the battlefield, but they are best viewed as fast and highly maneuverable *vehicles* which give today's commanders a new mobility which has transformed traditional military operations out of all recognition.

◁ The Soviet Antonov An-124 "Condor", the largest aircraft in the world, which is marginally bigger than the C-5 Galaxy with a reputedly better rough field performance. Like the Galaxy it has an upward-pivoting nose and rear ramp door. The Soviet equivalent of the Hercules is the An-12 "Cub." **Speed**: 535mph **Range**: 10,250mi **Max payload**: 33,065lb.

◁ An RAF C-130 Hercules (inset). Note the inflight refueling probe fitted above the cockpit. Air-to-air refueling is a vital element in modern air operations. The most widely used of all military transports, the Hercules is remarkably agile for an aircraft its size. There are many Hercules variants, including minelayers, maritime patrol, models, tankers, gunships, communications and ECM platforms and special operations versions. **Main picture**: A Black Hawk helicopter is loaded on to a Hercules. **Speed**: 375mph **Range**: 4,895mi **Ceiling**: 33,000ft **Max payload**: 42,680lb.

# SEA POWER

*In the 1950s the change to high-performance jets required a big increase in the size of aircraft carriers. Today the big Conventional Takeoff and Landing (CTOL) carrier remains the most important instrument of air power at sea.*

## CAPITAL SHIPS

The USS *Nimitz*, commissioned in 1975, displaces over 90,000 tons, is just under 1,090ft long and carries 100 aircraft. With her nuclear powerplant the carrier's range and independence increases dramatically. The U.S. Navy currently deploys 15 "super-carriers" equipped with a range of specialized aircraft which can provide tactical air support over a fleet at sea, support an amphibious landing or carry strike power to a distant enemy. The Royal Navy has opted for the V/STOL carrier carrying a mix of Sea Harriers and Sea King helicopters, while the Soviets have helicopter-carrying carriers of the "Kiev" class, which also fly V/STOL aircraft for reconnaissance.

The U.S. has recently refitted four "Iowa" class World War II battleships, the last of which, the USS *Wisconsin*, was recommisioned in 1988. Although her 16in primary guns and 5in secondary armament belong to a previous age of naval power, *Wisconsin*'s Tomahawk cruise missiles and Phalanx guns are in the forefront of military technology

▽ A salvo from the 16in guns of World War II battleship USS *Wisconsin*. **Displacement**: 58,000 tons **Complement**: 1,606 **Armament**: nine 16in guns, 20 5in guns, four Phalanx 20mm close-in weapon systems (CIWS) rotary cannon, eight Tomahawk cruise missile launchers, eight Harpoon antiship missile launchers.

◁ The USS *Nimitz*, built to survive in an all-out nuclear war and capable of delivering its own nuclear strike – against submarine or land targets – with over 100 nuclear weapons in its magazine. However, the size and striking power of the CTOL make it a prime target in any war, and it remains particularly vulnerable to submarine and missile attack.
**Displacement**: 91,487 tons
**Length**: 1,092ft **Speed**: 35kts
**Armament**: four 20 mm Phalanx close-in weapon systems (CIWS)
**Aircraft**: approx. 90 **Complement**: 3,000 plus 3,000 air group.

△ HMS *Invincible*, originally designed to operate large ASW helicopters, was modified to carry Sea Harrier aircraft. Note the white dome of the Phalanx 20mm CIWS at the aft end of the deck and the seven-degree "ski-jump" which enables the Harriers to take off with a greater payload in a shorter length.
**Displacement**: 16,256 tons
**Length**: 675ft **Complement**: 1,000 plus 320 air group **Armament**: one twin Sea Dart launcher, two Phalanx CIWS **Aircraft**: five Sea Harriers, 11 Sea Kings (in Falklands 10 Sea Harriers).

Figures in brackets denote standard complement for strike carrier, which will also carry tankers and utility aircraft.

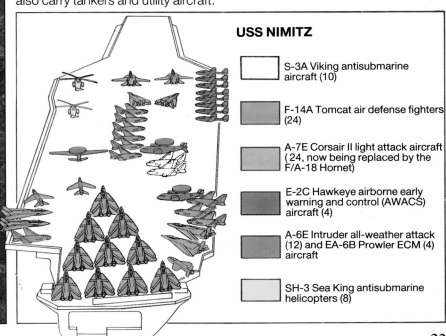

## USS NIMITZ

S-3A Viking antisubmarine aircraft (10)

F-14A Tomcat air defense fighters (24)

A-7E Corsair II light attack aircraft (24, now being replaced by the F/A-18 Hornet)

E-2C Hawkeye airborne early warning and control (AWACS) aircraft (4)

A-6E Intruder all-weather attack (12) and EA-6B Prowler ECM (4) aircraft

SH-3 Sea King antisubmarine helicopters (8)

# SEA POWER

## THE BATTLE FLEET

With the exception of aircraft carriers, the largest warships built since World War II are the Soviet nuclear-powered "Kirov" class battlecruisers, which displaced over 30,000 tons and are armed with a formidable mix of SSMs, SAMs and ASW weapons. "Missile cruisers" perform a variety of roles. The American nuclear-powered "California" class cruisers act as carrier escorts, forming part of the battle group screen against air and submarine attack. They carry a wide range of antiship, antiaircraft and antisubmarine weapons: among them Tomahawk surface-to-surface missiles and antisubmarine rocket (ASROC) missiles armed with a nuclear depth charge.

Also attached to the battle fleet are destroyers, frigates, minehunters, and auxiliary vessels carrying fuel and supplies.

◁ The Type 22 "Broadsword" class frigate HMS *Brave*'s Lynx helicopter lifts off during the Gulf War. The versatile Lynx can handle the principal tasks of a modern naval helicopter: antisubmarine operations, vertical replenishment (vertrep) and, armed with its four Sea Skua antiship missiles, surface strike. The helicopter has become an important naval asset and a helicopter platform and hangarage are now essential aspects of warship design, allowing even patrol boats to have their own air support. Like most naval helicopters, the Lynx retains wheels, convenient for maneuvering it into its hanger by manpower.

A Type 22 frigate like HMS *Brave* is considerably bigger than some warships rated as destroyers. **Displacement**: 4,400 tons (fully loaded) **Length**: 430ft **Speed**: 29 knts **Main aramament**: MM 38 Exocet SSms, GWS25 Sea Wolf SAMs **Aircraft**: two Lynx antiship helicopters **Complement**: 248 (max)

◁ The USS *California*, a nuclear-powered guided-missile cruiser whose principal role is to provide a carrier battle group with antiaircraft defense. **Displacement**: 11,100 tons (full load) **Length**: 596ft **Beam**: 61ft **Speed**: 39 knots **Main Armament**: two quadruple Tomahawk SSM launchers, two quadruple Harpoon SSM launchers, two SM2-MR SAM launchers (80 missiles), one octuple ASROC launcher (24 missiles).

Mines still play an important part in naval warfare. The Royal Navy's "Hunt" class coastal minehunter is the largest GRP-hulled ship in the world. Its Glassfiber Reinforced Plastic hull helps it to present as low as "signature" as possible to mine activation systems.

Destruction of Mines
**1** Cutting: sharp wire severs bottom-tethered mines.
**2** Exploding: towed device emits acoustic or magnetic signal to explode mine.
**3** Undersea robot (see below)

PAP-104
The "Hunt" class carries the French PAP-104 system, consisting of two battery-powered, wire-guided remotely controlled submersibles which can be maneuvered alongside the target mine to deal with it. The PAP has an onboard TV camera.

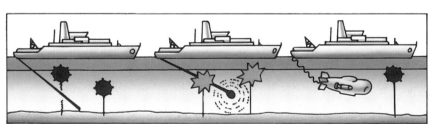

**1** Against "bottom" mines: PAP drops explosive charge near mine with timed fuse.
**2** Against tethered mine: PAP is fitted with front and side cable cutters.
**3**: Any mine: PAP fitted with manipulator arm clamps explosive charge to tether.

## SUBMARINES

The world's first nuclear-powered submarine, USS *Nautilus*, launched in 1954, revolutionized naval warfare. Today's SSBNs (nuclear-powered ballistic missile submarines) of the U.S. "Ohio" and Soviet "Typhoon" class are the most powerful warships in service. It has been said that a single "Ohio" class boat is the third largest nuclear power in the world. Essentially they are underwater missile silos, difficult to detect and capable of remaining submerged for months at a time, and armed with extremely accurate missiles, each of which has a number of independently targeted warheads.

The most effective single weapon for detecting and attacking an enemy submarine is another submarine – the "hunter-killer" – usually a nuclear-powered submarine (SSN). The guided-missile-firing nuclear-powered attack submarine is also a deadly enemy of the surface ship, able to cripple a "high value" target, for example an aircraft carrier, not only with torpedoes but also with a salvo of cruise missiles. Since 1959 the U.S. submarine program has been all-nuclear, but there is still an important role for conventionally powered submarines in the world's navies.

▽ The USS *Ohio*, mainstay of the U.S. SSBN fleet in the 1990s. The "teardrop"-shaped hull of the modern submarine means poor surface handling but makes it faster and more maneuverable beneath the surface, enabling it to be literally "flown" through the water to outrun many surface warships. Designed to stay submerged for long periods, the "Ohio" class SSBNs carry the multi-warhead Trident missile which has a range of 4,350mi.
**Displacement**: 16,764 tons (surfaced) **Length**: 560ft **Beam**: 42ft
**Speed**: 20 knots (surfaced), 24 knots (dived) **Max diving depth**: 1640ft **Armament**: 24 launch tubes for Trident D5 II ballistic missiles and four 533mm bow tubes
**Complement**: 133

◁ The Soviet "Typhoon" class SSBN, whose unusual hull form is almost double the beam of the USS "Ohio" class. A menacing monster of the deep, the *Typhoon* has been designed to operate under the polar ice cap. It can accommodate missiles capable of hitting the continental U.S.A. without leaving northern Soviet waters. Like its USS "Ohio" class equivalent, the *Typhoon* carries ballistic missiles with multiple warheads, known as MIRV (Mulitple Independently-Targetable Reentry Vehicles). **Displacement**: 26,000 tons (surfaced) **Length**: 557ft **Beam**: 75ft **Speed**: 20 knots (surfaced), 30 knots (dived) **Max diving depth**: 1,968ft **Armament**: 20 launch tubes for 20 SS-N-20 ballistic missiles and six 533mm bow torpedo tubes **Complement**: 150

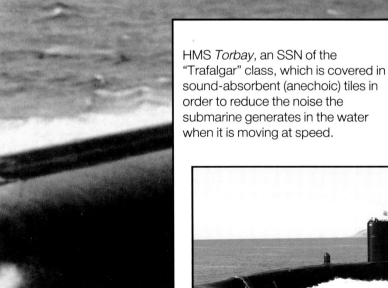

HMS *Torbay*, an SSN of the "Trafalgar" class, which is covered in sound-absorbent (anechoic) tiles in order to reduce the noise the submarine generates in the water when it is moving at speed.

**Displacement**: 4,200 tons (surfaced) **Length**: 280ft **Beam**: 32ft **Speed**: 32 knots (dived) **Armament**: Sub-Harpoon antiship missiles, plus five 533mm bow torpedo tubes **Complement**: 130

# MISSILES AND SMART WEAPONS

*Modern missile systems range from the Intercontinental Ballistic Missile (ICBM) to the human-portable antitank weapon in the hands of the individual infantryman. They provide both offensive and defensive capability.*

## MISSILES

The ranges of missiles are greater than those of conventional artillery and in terms of "kills" per round they are cost-effective. The American AIM-54 Phoenix long-range air-to-air missile, carried by the carrier-borne F-14 Tomcat fighter, costs $300,000 but it can destroy a strategic bomber.

The Phoenix is a "fire-and-forget" missile. It is given its initial instructions by the Tomcat's radar and weapons control system, and then flies to a computer-predicted point in the sky. About 12mi from the target it switches on its own small onboard radar for "terminal guidance" to the target. Once the Phoenix is launched, the Tomcat can break away. The Tomcat's radar can pick up targets at ranges of 155mi and track 24 at once while engaging six simultaneously.

▷ The MIM-104 Patriot missile was originally designed to intercept low-flying aircraft, but in the Gulf War it was used with great success as an antimissile missile against Iraqi Scud B rockets fired at targets in Israel and Saudi Arabia. A Patriot battery contains up to three launchers which in turn house four missiles. In the battery are an electrical supply truck, a ground radar vehicle and an engagement control center, the only manned part of the unit. At the heart of the system is the MPQ-53 phased-array radar, which relays details of course, speed, and possible type of incoming missiles to the engagement control center. The process is almost wholly automated.

◁ In the delivery of strategic nuclear weapons the missile remains supreme. Nuclear ordnance from guns and aircraft can be used tactically, but nuclear "deterrence" has been maintained by land-based missile delivery systems, often hidden in reinforced concrete silos, and by sea-based systems carried in two SSBBs. Left: The land-based U.S. Peacekeeper ICBM (formerly known as MX), which can deliver 10 independently targeted 330-kiloton warheads over a range of 6,800mi. A kiloton is the equivalent of the explosive force of 1,000 tons of high-explosive charge.

## PATRIOT MISSILE

**1** Main phased-array radar detects and tracks target Scud. Patriot missile is launched.

**2** Patriot receives reflected radar signals from the target.

**3** Patriot returns signal to ground station.

**4** Ground control guides missile on to most efficient track to target. Patriot closes with target, proximity fuse detonates, destroying Scud.

In the Gulf War approximately 140 Patriots were launched from sites in Saudi Arabia and Israel.

# MISSILES AND SMART WEAPONS

## SMART WEAPONS

During the Gulf War much attention was devoted to so-called "smart weapons," although they accounted for only seven percent of the tens of thousands of tons of ordnance dropped on Iraq and Kuwait. A laser designator can give a "smart" capability to conventional free-fall bombs equipped with a laser seeker. The seeker picks up the laser energy reflected from a target "illuminated" by a pencil-thin laser beam directed at it by another aircraft or ground designator. A target pinpointed in this way becomes a beacon for any weapon with a laser seeker in its nose. Today the number of laser-guided weapons has grown to include powered air-to-surface munitions like the AGM-65 Maverick, carried by the A-10 attack aircraft, the helicopter-launched AGM-114 Hellfire and artillery shells like the M712 Copperhead. Among the new antitank submunitions is the American Skeet, carried in the warhead of the Standoff Tactical Missile, which can be fired over a range of 250mi. When it is released over the target the Skeet – a bomblet weighing about 4.5lb and carrying a 1lb warhead – locates an armored vehicle with an infrared sensor and then fires the warhead.

▽ A modern cruise missile can carry a nuclear or conventional warhead, flying low and relatively slowly over thousands of miles delivering it within 100ft of the target. Essentially the air-breathing cruise is a small (20ft long) unmanned aircraft piloted by an ultrasophisticated computer (see below). During the Gulf War approximately 285 General Dynamics BGM-109 sea-launched cruise missiles were fired by U.S. warships.

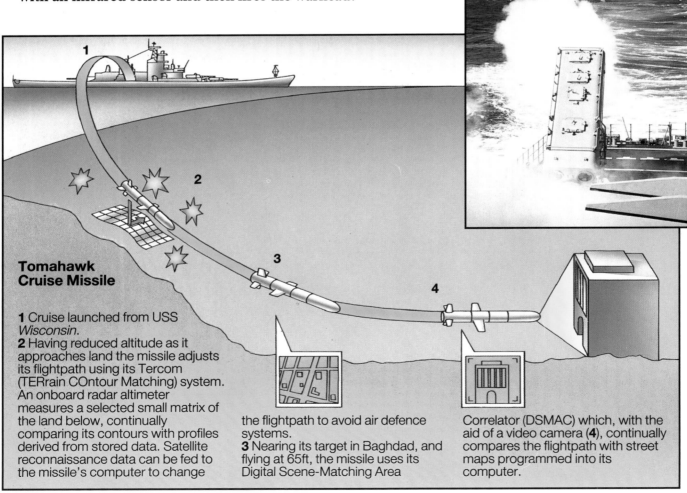

**Tomahawk Cruise Missile**

**1** Cruise launched from USS *Wisconsin*.
**2** Having reduced altitude as it approaches land the missile adjusts its flightpath using its Tercom (TERrain COntour Matching) system. An onboard radar altimeter measures a selected small matrix of the land below, continually comparing its contours with profiles derived from stored data. Satellite reconnaissance data can be fed to the missile's computer to change the flightpath to avoid air defence systems.
**3** Nearing its target in Baghdad, and flying at 65ft, the missile uses its Digital Scene-Matching Area Correlator (DSMAC) which, with the aid of a video camera (**4**), continually compares the flightpath with street maps programmed into its computer.

# GLOSSARY

**AAM** – air-to-air missile. A typical example is the American short-range AIM9 Sidewinder series.

**Active terminal homing** – applied to a missile or munition which uses an onboard system to guide it to the target during the last phase of its flight.

**ALCM** – air-launched cruise missile.

**AMRAAM** – advanced medium-range AAM which uses an onboard radar to locate its target during the last phase of its flight.

**ASROC** – American Anti-Submarine ROCket, fired from warships and equipped with a nuclear warhead which explodes at an appropriate depth to destroy a submarine. SUBROC (SUBmarine-launched ROCket) is carried by U.S. hunter-killer submarines and is launched from a torpedo tube.

**ASW** – antisubmarine warfare

**ATM** – antitank missile

**Avionics** – aviation electronics

**CIWS** – close-in-weapon system. A fast-slewing, rapid-firing rotary cannon which provides warships with point defense against sea-skimming missiles.

**Copperhead** – an antitank projectile fired from a 155mm gun and laser-guided to the target.

**Depleted uranium** – nonradioactive uranium

**ECM** – electronic countermeasures.

**FBW** – fly-by-wire

**Fire and forget** – a missile equipped with midflight **inertial**

**guidance** and **active terminal homing** or a heat-seeking missile which does not require target illumination or guidance commands from the launch aircraft once launched.

**FLIR** – forward-looking infrared. Electro-optical night and "all-weather" vision equipment standard on modern fighter-bombers and attack helicopters like the AH-64A Apache.

**ICBM** – intercontinental ballistic missile

**IHADSS** – Integrated Helmet And Display Sighting System, which projects information into the line of sight of the crew of the AH-64A Apache attack helicopter via a monocle attached to the flight helmet.

**Improved Conventional Munitions (ICMs)** – a new generation of guided and cargo-carrying artillery projectiles of which Copperhead is an example.

**JP 233** – a weapon carried by the Tornado attack aircraft which uses small cratering mines and delayed action mines to take out enemy runways.

**Inertial guidance** – system of gyroscopes and accelerometers which keeps a missile on a programmed heading.

**Maverick** – American laser- or infrared-guided air-to-surface missile (ASM).

**MLRS** – Multiple Launch Rocket System

**MX** – Missile eXperimental

**NBC** – Nuclear, Biological, Chemical

**Phased-array radar** – an advanced radar using a fixed flat area consisting of many aerials instead of a single large rotating aerial and capable of following hundreds of targets at great distances.

**Pulse-Doppler radar** – a radar which by identifying the Doppler shift of radar pulses reflected by a low-flying enemy can confer a "look down/shoot down" capability.

**SAM** – surface-to-air missile

**Smart** – slang expression applied to weapon systems which possess a large measure of onboard autonomous guidance, for example laser-guided bombs (LGBs).

**SSM** – surface-to-surface missile

**SSBN** – submarine, ballistic-missile, nuclear-powered

**SSN** – submarine, attack, nuclear-powered

**TERCOM** – TERrain COntour Matching. System carried by a cruise missile which uses a computer to compare the terrain below with a pre-programmed flight plan.

**V/STOL** – vertical/short takeoff and landing.

# INDEX

## PHOTO CREDITS

Cover left top and bottom, title page and pages 2-3, 8 bottom, 10 bottom, 11 top and bottom, 18 middle, 18 top, 20, 21 bottom inset, 23 and 24: Photo Press Defence Picture Library; cover right and page 29: Raytheon Company; pages 4-5, 10 top, 13 middle, 14, 21 top and middle, 25 top and bottom, 28 and 30: TRH Pictures; pages 5 middle, 7 middle and 17 middle: British Crown Copyright/MOD reproduced with the permission of the Controller or Her Britannic Majesty's Stationary Office; pages 5 bottom, 7 top, 8 top, 9 top and bottom, 12-13 12, 15 top, 16 top and bottom, 22, 22-23, 26-27 and 27 top: Department of Defense Washington D.C. USA; pages 6 and 7 bottom: Lt. Col. THE Fouldes; pages 13 bottom, 15 bottom, 17 top, 19 bottom and 21 bottom: Jane's Information Group; page 27: VSEL.